Just Different

Author & Illustrated by: Laura L. Vercillo

Just Different Book Series
WWW.PacedPatience.com

Dedicated to my kids.
You are all my kids.

Thank God for inspiring me for a wonderful purpose in life.

I would like to thank Audrey Vercillo, without you this would be another social story at my desk. Thank you for your encouragement and support.

Thank you to LWS teachers and staff who encourage, review and edit my stories.

Thank you to my family; Randy, Zach , Tyler and my mom for being patient with me while I work on the "next" story.

This story is designed to be read aloud in class or can be read to yourself. The purpose of this story, and Just Different

Series, is to reach out and help educate people of all abilities. We are all different. Our brains work differently. There is no right or wrong. There is no "normal." Please encourage for all to have empathy, understanding and most importantly, be kind.

We are all just different.

"Mrs. Owl, why does Mrs. Peacock play games with Bluie? " asked T-Bird.

"Play games?" asked Mrs. Owl.

"Yes, he takes breaks and plays with toys." said T-Bird.

"Well T-Bird, maybe we should talk about that. You know how we are all made differently?" asked Mrs. Owl.

"Yes, I know that." answered T-Bird.

"We look different, but we are also made differently on the outside and on the inside. Sometimes our brains work differently then others." Mrs. Owl chirped.

"Our insides are different? I don't understand." asked T-Bird.

"Well, sometimes our insides work a little different,

which make our outsides work a little different. My ears can hear stronger than yours do. Finchie has a weak wing and flies differently.." Mrs. Owl explained.

"Sometimes our insides are the same, but they work differently. Sometimes our brains may work differently. You may be great at catching worms, but others need help catching worms.." explained Mrs. Owl.

Some of us might chirp at the wrong time. Our chirps sound different. Some of us fly too close to another. Some fly different. We are all different. Different is okay. It doesn't make it wrong.

It doesn't make it right.

It just makes us different.." Mrs. Owl tweeted.

"Oh, like Parakeet. She keeps saying the same thing over and over. I get so tired of it already. Come on, enough!"
T-Bird stated.

"Exactly. I know it can be very frustrating sometimes. It is not always easy to be patient and understanding. What do you say to Parakeet when she keeps repeating herself?" asked Mrs. Owl.

"I don't say anything. I don't know what to say. It's kind of different. I know others tell her to stop it or be quiet, they pick on her." T-Bird whispered.

"Hmm, how does that make you feel when you hear them talk to Parakeet like that?" Mrs. Owl questioned.

"I don't know, she is different. I guess I don't feel anything." replied T-Bird.

"How does Parakeet seem to feel? Do you know?" asked
Mrs. Owl.

"I don't know, probably sad or maybe mad? She does look
lonely." said T-Bird.

"T-Bird, what if your dad repeated himself like Parakeet? Would you be upset if others laughed at him? What if they ran away from you mom, or didn't want to stand next to her?"

Mrs. Owl asked.

"Wow, I don't know. My mom and dad aren't different like that." said T-Bird.

"We are just pretending 'what if' how would that make you feel?" asked Mrs. Owl.

"I guess I would be upset. I might be embarrassed, even mad. It would be really rude!" answered T-Bird.

"We are all different, we act, talk, think and move differently. Parakeet and Bluie are just two of many friends that are

different. Different is not right or wrong. Different is okay. Different is just different. Different doesn't change you." hooted Mrs. Owl.

T-Bird asked, "Why do they want to be different? Why can't they be normal. Why can't they just be like us? "

"Great question, Mrs. Owl responded, if only it were that easy. First, what is normal? They have to really work hard at doing the things that may be easy for us. Getting worms is easy for us,

but not easy for everyone. There are things that are hard for us and may be easy for them. It's not a choice. Remember, we are different. Different is normal. Different doesn't change you. Who decides what is normal?

"But it's just getting worms. There is nothing hard about that!" said T-Bird.

"Let me explain it this way. T-Bird, make a nest."

"What do you mean? I can't make a nest by myself. I just can't do that by myself." T-Bird exclaimed.

"Exactly, that is hard for you. That is why Bluie needs

Mrs. Peacock. She helps teach him to do things that are harder for him." said Mrs. Owl.

"You have seen your mom make a nest, but you cannot make one on your own. In time, you might be able to. You might not. We all have different abilities. We all have different challenges." said Mrs. Owl.

T-Bird replied, "I think I am starting to understand. What is easy for me, isn't easy for others. What is hard for me, isn't hard for others. We are all different. Different is okay. Different is not right or wrong, it's just different. But why do they get to play with toys?"

"Ah, the fidgets. It looks like playing, but fidgets are used to help us learn and work hard. Working hard can be fun. The fidgets are tools. Tools help them learn in a fun way. Sometimes fidgets help focus better." Mrs. Owl answered.

"I think I should be nicer to Parakeet. Parakeet is different. She is okay. Different is okay. Different doesn't change us." said T-Bird.

"T-Bird, you are really growing up. I am proud of you. I know it's not easy to be patient or understand different, but it's important that we do our best and be kind.." Mrs. Owl said.

"There is nothing wrong with needing help. You need help to do the things that you struggle with or need a little guidance." Mrs. Owl wisely rasped.

"Mrs. Owl, you are so wise. We are different on the outside. We are also different on the inside. No wrong or right. Just different. When we are respectful and kind, our hearts grow bigger." piped T-Bird.

"Mrs. Peacock is a teacher who helps those who need help. She is called a paraprofessional. She helps the teacher and she helps students who need help."

"Maybe I can help Bluie or Parakeet sometimes too."
said T-Bird.

"That would be so wonderful. I am glad you are understanding and wanting to be helpful. I know bluie and Parakeet will be happy too!."
said Mrs. Owl.

Maybe you know someone that is different. Maybe they do things different. It not okay to make fun of anyone who is different. Making fun of anyone is being a bully. There is no right or wrong. Different is okay. Different doesn't change who you are. Different is just different. Always be safe, respectful and responsible. Always be kind.

This book is over. I hope you liked it! Tell all your friends about this book! Tell all your friends about this book! Tell all your friends about this book!

Tell..................

The End

Other Books by this Author: Laura L. Vercillo - WWW.PacedPatience.Com

Available for purchase on Amazon.com
Teacherspayteachers.com/store/paced-patience
www.etsy.com/shop/lvercillo
Www.facebook.com/pacedpatience

* Christian reference books